A CENTURY OF
MOTORING

Published in Great Britain in 2015 by Shire Publications Ltd, PO Box 883, Oxford, OX1 9PL, UK.

PO Box 3985, New York, NY 10185-3985, USA.

E-mail: shire@shirebooks.co.uk   www.shirebooks.co.uk

A CIP catalogue record for this book is available from the British Library.

Shire Century no. 4.   ISBN-13: 978 0 74781 510 5

PDF e-book ISBN: 978 1 78442 066 6

ePub ISBN: 978 1 78442 065 9

Jon Pressnell has asserted his right under the Copyright, Designs and Patents Act, 1988, to be identified as the author of this book.

Designed by Stewart Larking and typeset in Swiss 721 and Adobe Garamond Pro.

Printed in China through Worldprint Ltd.

15 16 17 18 19   10 9 8 7 6 5 4 3 2 1

A CENTURY OF
MOTORING

JON PRESSNELL

CONTENTS

INTRODUCTION

The first motor car arrived in the British Isles in 1895. Within a year the permitted speed for these new devices was raised from 4 mph to 12 mph. Whether known as an autocar, an automobile, a motor, or simply as a car, the machines were initially little more than playthings for the rich – and as such encountered much popular and press hostility. In 1904 registration numbers and driving licences were introduced, along with a 20 mph speed limit.

By 1914 the motor car had taken its definitive form. Tiller steering had at last disappeared in 1911; the front-engined, rear-wheel-drive *système Panhard* was almost universal; coachwork was moving away decisively from its horse-carriage roots; electric lighting was increasingly a regular fitting; even unit construction of body and chassis was being essayed. At the same time a new industry was forming, with mass-production by Ford and Morris poised to drive car-ownership upwards – aided by new lower-cost cyclecars and light cars. Meanwhile British car and commercial production had risen from 12,000 vehicles in 1907 to 44,000 in 1913.

The First World War was to be the first motorised conflict, and one that would see a generation of soldiers gaining experience of the automobile. With the end of hostilities, motoring took off. In 1914 there had been 132,000 cars in Britain; this figure rose to 242,500 in 1921, and by 1924 there were four times as many cars on the road as in 1919. Numbers continued to climb, until in 1939 total registrations hit the 2 million mark.

Talk of 'cars for everyman' was fanciful, however. In the inter-war years the cost of a car decreased sharply in real terms, both because prices were being reduced and because earnings were increasing. But in 1934 *The Economist* calculated that an annual income of approaching £400 was still needed to run a car, at a time when the average annual wage was less than half that figure. Unsurprisingly, motorcycles accounted for roughly 40 per cent of private vehicles at the time.

The impact of the motor car was considerable. Cars opened up the country. Motor touring led to the discovery of rural England by town dwellers. Holidaymakers and daytrippers transformed coastal areas – and even more so when they chose to build holiday or retirement homes, leading to rashes of bungalow developments and so-called 'shanty towns'. Cars also allowed people to live in the country, or outside town in one of the new suburbs, and to drive to work or to the station from which they could commute to town. Arterial roads out of major towns led to 'ribbon development' alongside the new highways.

Post-war, the democratisation of the motor car was slow. In 1955 one household in five had a car, but among households termed 'working class' the figure was one in fourteen. Ten years later, the figures were respectively two in five and one in five. Today, car ownership is universal, and by the turn of the millennium there were over 25 million private cars registered in the United Kingdom.

Dressing for the motor car

While the gradual disappearance of open-cockpit coachwork had lessened exposure to the elements, it was still necessary in Edwardian times for motorists to be appropriately garbed. This was not just because cars were generally open-bodied, with the occupants sitting high and unsheltered, but also because of the dust raised on the unsealed roads of the time.

The wealthy went to suppliers such as Dunhill, Burberry or Aquascutum, or had their tailor or milliner confect suitable items. A sturdy coat, long and usually double-breasted, was a basic requirement. Leather was one choice, as it was windproof, but breathable materials such as tweed and Irish frieze (a coarse-woven woollen cloth) were also popular, as were proofed coats in gabardine (invented by Burberry) or aquascutum (a waterproof wool which gave its name to the eponymous company).

Coats were likely to be fur-lined and possibly fur-trimmed, sometimes in exotic furs such as puma, opossum, seal or leopard. Coats wholly of fur were also seen, but held dust and were unpleasant in the wet. A leather waistcoat might be worn underneath, and gloves, goggles and a cap (often with ear-flaps) were vital items of equipment.

Ladies protected their heads with hoods, perhaps equipped with mica or silicone visors, or covered hat and face with a veil. Full-face masks were sufficiently bizarre to be a minority interest. Feet, meanwhile, might be kept warm by fur overboots or foot muffs, accompanied by a fur knee apron for the lower body, and maybe even a pair of leather motoring knickers.

Model T with staff of Ford's London office

If by the outbreak of the First World War one car could be said to have started the long haul to popularising motoring in Britain, it had to be the Ford, British assembly of which had begun in 1911. The reasons why British motorists took to the Model T were simple. Mass-production methods, as pioneered by Ford in the US, meant that it was cheap: at £135 in 1914 for a four-seat tourer, it cost £40 less than the first Morris Oxford. Crucially, too, it was light but robust, and made of high-quality metals. It had a two-speed transmission with gear engagement by pedal, and with its low-stressed 2890cc four-cylinder engine it was capable of good performance for the time, with a maximum speed of just over 40 mph.

Initially the Ford was sneered at by many, who regarded a hand-assembled British motor car as being the only motorised transport suitable for gentlefolk. Such arguments did not last long, and by 1919 a full 41 per cent of cars on the roads were Fords. Motoring magazines devoted special sections to the Model T, and countless firms offered accessories to improve or embellish the car.

Inevitably, though, Ford's dominance started to be eroded as the car became more old-fashioned. The Model T was also dealt a blow by the 1921 revision of the horsepower tax, a change specifically intended to deter the purchase of cars of American origin with large-bore engines; despite this, only in 1924 did Ford lose market leadership.

GN cyclecar in Regents Park, London

In the years immediately before the First World War a new form of minimalist motoring arrived, in the form of the cyclecar. Using a motorcycle engine, or similar, and often driven by a chain or belt to the rear wheels, they were lightweight, crude, and frequently of eccentric design; one, indeed, the French Bédélia, went so far as to seat the passenger in front of the driver.

Such vehicles had the virtue of being cheaper than a conventional car, but were not, however, the only game in town. For those who could afford a little more, another new breed of vehicle was the so-called 'light car' – literally a shrunken version of an orthodox car and powered by an engine of around a litre in capacity. The model that rose to prominence in this category, following its 1913 announcement, was the 1018cc Morris Oxford.

Astonishing as it may seem, leisure motoring continued to be permitted well into the First World War; indeed, the motoring community felt grievously offended by any suggestion that it might be a morally questionable extravagance at such a time. Motorists were doing their patriotic duty and helping the war effort, it was maintained, by having a car in which to drive wounded soldiers to tea. It was only in November 1917 that petrol was rationed. That same year the import of motor vehicles was banned, domestic manufacture having largely dried up as car-makers turned to making munitions and the like.

Filling with Shell at a Clapham garage

Early motorists had to buy petrol from the chemist, but soon cycle and motor engineers, ironmongers and other shopkeepers started to stock the fuel. In 1899 Pratt's, the antecedent of Esso, introduced two-gallon cans, and these become the norm, stipulated by law.

The first petrol pump arrived in 1915, but at this stage there was no such thing as a filling station. In 1919 the AA opened the first, in a pre-fabricated timber hut, equipped with a pump from 1920. That same year Pratt's started selling petrol from pumps, and Shell soon followed. In 1921 the former opened the first commercial drive-in facility, by London's Battersea Bridge.

Immediately after the First World War these two companies dominated the market, Shell with a 51 per cent share and Pratt's 37 per cent. In 1935 Pratt's was re-named Esso. Meanwhile, lead in petrol arrived in 1928, and allowed higher-compression engines by eliminating 'knocking' under load; octane levels were low, however, with the best pre-war fuel having an 80–82 rating.

The changeover from cans to pumps took place progressively during the 1920s, fuel companies lending money so garages could install underground tanks. By 1929 there were 28,000 retail outlets, with an average of two pumps each; by the 1930s these had become electric – rather than handle-operated, as in this photo. The establishment shown also offers hire cars – quite possibly with a driver, as was sometimes the practice – as well as garaging for up to a hundred cars.

Chums in a 'Chummy' Austin

These revellers are perched on a very early example of an Austin Seven, with tourer coachwork of the type nicknamed 'Chummy'. Many people found the little Austin hard to take seriously, on account of its small size, and it was the subject of countless cartoons and music-hall jokes. It was however a highly significant car in the history of British motoring. Industrially, it saved Austin from collapse, and made a wealthy man of Sir Herbert Austin. More importantly, it introduced generations of Britons to the motor car, and sounded the death-knell for the sundry gimcrack cyclecars that had represented minimalist motoring before the Austin came along.

The Austin had its conceptual eccentricities, but it was a real car in miniature, with a four-cylinder engine, four-wheel brakes (when such things were by no means normal), and seating – just – for four people. Equally to the point, it was constructed of good-quality materials. Made from 1922 until 1939, to the same mechanical configuration but with progressive updates to the body, a total of nearly 300,000 were manufactured.

Sevens continued to give sterling service to marginal motorists up until the arrival of roadworthiness testing in 1961. Post-war, many were rebuilt into low-cost racing cars or roadgoing 'specials'. Today, helped by lively clubs and a good supply of spares, the Seven continues to be hugely popular in the world of classic cars, and has introduced many a youngster to the joys of vintage and post-vintage motoring.

Picnic at Brooklands race track

Brooklands, situated in Weybridge, Surrey, and opened in 1907, was one of the world's first purpose-built race tracks, and is regarded as being the cradle of British motor sport. Its banked circuit constituted a major engineering feat and added to the drama of racing – and its danger, as testified by several deaths over the years. Within the track was an airfield and associated facilities. Many early aircraft were built and tested at the site, and after the Second World War Brooklands became a facility for the Vickers aircraft business.

Motor racing between the wars was very much the preserve of an elite of moneyed amateurs, and Brooklands was an important part of the calendar for the well-to-do of southern England – complete with on-site bookmakers, and betting as at a horse-race. Indeed, *Motor Sport* magazine spoke of a 'Country Club atmosphere' at the track. The slogan associated with Brooklands, 'The Right Crowd and No Crowding', gives a flavour of the social reality behind the romanticising of nostalgia-afflicted enthusiasts. One reflection of this was that the British Motor Cycle Racing Club had its own bar and restaurant, and a separate entrance to the Clubhouse, as the motorcyclists were tacitly regarded as coming from an inferior class. As for women, it was only in 1936 that they were allowed to compete on the same terms as men.

The car in the photo is a Standard with two-seat open coachwork incorporating a dickey seat behind the cockpit – the cheapest type of bodywork in the 1920s.

Chauffeur-driven Rolls-Royce at Le Touquet

circa 1925

Chauffeurs had been a common part of motoring in the very early days; not just driving the cars, they looked after their capricious mechanicals and ensured their presentation was always immaculate. This, and the fact of accompanying their employer on journeys, gave them a position high up the pecking order of domestic servants.

In the inter-war years it was still not unusual for wealthy motorists to have a driver in their employ – all the more so if they had a sizeable luxury motor car such as the Rolls-Royce in this photo. Indeed, such a chauffeur would quite likely have passed through the Rolls-Royce School of Instruction, the company's chauffeur-training arm. Even the prosperous middle classes might have recourse to a chauffeur: someone in senior management, for example, might not have a car of his own, but might have his firm's chauffeur collect him from home each morning in the company's Austin or Humber. Chauffeurs were invariably male – it would never have occurred to an employer to think otherwise – and they would dress in a double-breasted uniform or latterly a lounge suit, with a cap.

All pre-1945 Rolls-Royces were sold in chassis form, with the buyer choosing how to have his new acquisition bodied by one of the many British coachbuilders. This particular car, a late example of the legendary Silver Ghost, carries landaulet coachwork: even well into the 1920s, more traditional body styles still evoked those found on horse-drawn carriages. The owner is Captain John Murdocke, a high-end tailor and fashion commentator.

Renault at Sennen Cove, Cornwall

Even in the 1920s many British roads outside towns and cities were unmade, with a loose macadam surface; in towns, wood-block or granite setts made life easier, although wood-block roads were notoriously slippery in the wet.

On unmade roads, dust was a major problem (as were punctures), and in the early days of motoring there was much experimentation with shielding of the wheels to avoid dust being thrown up; as mentioned earlier, one also had to dress appropriately.

Tarmac, achieved by mixing tar with aggregate, was patented in 1901. The Automobile Association (AA) and the Royal Automobile Club (RAC) pressed local authorities to resurface roads in tarmac, and a further fillip was the introduction of taxation of motor vehicles and petrol in 1909: for a while the revenue from this Road Fund was ring-fenced and spent expressly on road improvements. The first 'raid' on this resource by a chancellor, to fund other expenditure, took place in 1926, and in 1936 hypothecation of the tax for use solely on roads was ended; the Road Fund, however, was only wound up in 1955. Meanwhile, in 1937 central government took over responsibility for trunk roads from the local authorities; by this stage Britain's roads were largely metalled.

Because of its temperature sensitivity, by the 1920s tarmac was largely supplanted by an aggregate using asphalt, a petroleum-derived binder also called bitumen. Later, especially with the construction of motorways, concrete became a favoured material, along with 'tar-and-chip' bituminous surface treatment for low-traffic roads.

The Prince of Wales travels to France

Travelling abroad was part of the adventure of motoring in the inter-war years. Until the mid-1930s crossing the Channel involved a hair-raising operation in which cars were hoisted on board ship one by one, on wheel-slings or platforms. This started to change in 1936, with the arrival of the first roll-on-roll-off ferries. Plying between Dover and Dunkirk, they had a capacity of just twenty-five vehicles.

Right up until the end of the 1950s, going abroad was not just a physical but an administrative rigmarole, with motorists having to obtain specific items of paperwork through either the AA or the RAC. It was only in 1958 that the requirement for this *carnet* of documentation was abandoned by most countries in Western Europe; its provision had been an important part of the activities of the two motoring organisations, who also oversaw the loading and unloading of members' cars at the relevant cross-channel ports.

The photo shows the newly acquired Burney Streamline of the Prince of Wales (later King Edward VIII) being winched on board a ship to France, in August 1931. The Prince was lauded as a keen motorist, and the left-field choice of the Burney can indeed only have been that of an enthusiast. Created by Sir Dennistoun Burney, the man behind the R100 airship, it was an extraordinary supposedly aerodynamic saloon, with a rear engine. Just twelve were made: the car was ludicrously expensive and a handful to drive.

The London Motor Show

If one couldn't afford a car, one could afford to dream. And where better to dream than at the annual Motor Show, a place of pilgrimage where you could see, and perhaps sit in, not only the car you might eventually own, but also the car you would never in a lifetime be able to buy?

For generations of children, too, the Motor Show was a formative experience. Going from stand to stand, asking harassed salesmen 'Got any catalogues, mister?' and returning home with carrier-bags full of brochures was part of growing up – complete with the tears when one got lost, and ended up on the knees of the nice lady on the RAC stand.

The first Motor Show was held at Crystal Palace in 1903, and for 1904 it moved to Olympia, in Kensington, where it remained until 1937, when it transferred to Earls Court; that year sixty-six manufacturers and thirty-three coachbuilders were on display. The last Earls Court Motor Show was held in 1976, ahead of a move to Birmingham's NEC in 1978. Since 2008 the event has not been held.

To the fore in this photo are the stands of Austin (on the left) and mid-ranking quality manufacturer Armstrong Siddeley (on the right); in the gallery above, as at Earls Court, can be found the accessory manufacturers.

To the hunt – by Morris Oxford

This charming artwork advertising the six-cylinder Morris Oxford perfectly captures the social tone of the time. Both the image and the accompanying copy are shrewdly aimed at the well-to-do professional classes who could afford the £275 demanded for the Sports Coupé version shown.

Meanwhile, according to the Morris in-house magazine the company's smallest car, the Minor, was within the reach of even the most modest purse: 'Any steady-going working man in regular employment should be able to maintain a Morris Minor and bring the delights of the open road to his family, while to those in rather better circumstances the running costs for the year will assuredly represent less than the expenditure on rail and bus fares for two persons over the same period'. This was wishful thinking. When the average annual wage was roughly £150 (about £8,000 in today's money), even the cheapest Minor, at £100 in 1932, was well beyond the reach of the ordinary man in the street.

Having come to market leadership with the Bullnose, which at one stage took 41 per cent of the British market, Sir William Morris – or Lord Nuffield, as he became in 1934 – was still the dominant force in British motoring, a position he had anchored by offering fixed-price parts and servicing, hire-purchase and insurance schemes, and above all a range of well-priced cars of honourable quality. In 1935 he would introduce what would become Britain's best-selling car of the late 1930s, the Eight.

here
shrewd
judges meet . . .
you find the Oxford

Caravanning by the river in Chertsey, Surrey

The first commercially manufactured touring caravans arrived at the beginning of the 1920s. By the end of the decade there was a certain vogue for caravanning, accompanied by much romanticising about 'gipsy joys' and the like. With the accelerated spread of motoring, the 1930s would see a boom in caravan use. The hobby received an additional boost with the development of caravan rallies and the creation of caravan clubs. A further fillip was the increasing press attention given to caravanning, with *The Autocar* introducing a regular column on the subject in 1932 and the first caravan magazine appearing a year later.

During the 1920s, British caravanners either camped 'wild', wherever there was a convenient spot for their caravan, or else asked permission of a farmer or landowner to set up in one of his fields. By the end of the following decade, formalised sites were springing up, and licensing arrived in 1936, proof of the movement's coming of age.

By the 1930s caravans had became more streamlined in shape, led by the beetle-backed Car Cruiser, as in this photo. After the war, housing shortages meant that the industry tended for many years to concentrate more on residential caravans, but by the mid-1950s the touring caravan had re-established itself: in 1954 the Caravan Club had a membership approaching 17,000. This figure was to double by the end of the decade, as a prelude to sales of caravans rocketing during the 1960s.

Deco detailing on an SSI tourer

What is today termed Art Deco spread to the automotive world during the 1930s. Some cars, such as the Chrysler Airflow and Singer Airstream, clearly owed their streamlined form and ornamentation to Deco trends. More commonly – and more prudently, given the British motorist's essential conservatism – manufacturers generally went no further than adopting Art Deco stylistic devices to the interior of their cars.

It tends to be forgotten that even the most banal of British cars of the later 1930s often had a real exuberance to their interior presentation. An example is the 10 hp to 25 hp series of Morrises launched in 1935. The exterior was modestly streamlined but the passenger compartment featured splendid sunburst motifs and a Bakelite instrument panel with square dials.

William Lyons of SS Cars had a shrewd understanding of how to dress up his products to look classier than the average – a skill he showed right from the start, when he was putting special 'Swallow' bodies on Austin Seven chassis. In 1932 he announced the first SS car, the rakish Standard-based SSI, and the photo shows the open tourer version of this model, featuring a truly flamboyant sunburst pattern extending across the entire door trim. In 1935 Lyons introduced the SS-Jaguar, the antecedent of the post-war Jaguars that cemented his reputation as a maker of stylish but well-priced motor cars.

Four-up in the first MG Midget

This happy party is crammed into the two-seat cockpit of an M-type MG Midget, and according to the caption on the back of the photo they have motored from their hotel for 'a cooling dip at a wayside swimming pool' at Ashtead, in Surrey. A growing interest in recreational swimming was fed by the spread of motoring, and outdoor lidos became a feature of the inter-war years, sometimes being incorporated into the roadhouses – a mix of bar-restaurant and leisure centre – that were built alongside many arterial roads in the inter-war years.

Announced in 1928, the 847cc M-type was one of Britain's first series-produced affordable sports cars, introducing many a young man to the joys of sporting open-top motoring – and indeed to motor sport, in many instances. Although in its early days the M-type was used at Brooklands, and even fielded at Le Mans, soon more specialist MGs came to be used for racing. Those who competed in the 'M' tended to use it more in the sundry less arduous trials organised by local motor clubs, national bodies such as the Motor Cycle Club, and indeed the MG Car Club itself, which was formed in 1930.

In essence a re-bodied and lightly tuned adaptation of the Morris Minor, the MG was current until 1932, by which time over 3,000 had been made. This example has a fabric body; steel panelling for the body's ash frame only came in for the final year of production. There was also a fixed-head coupé version, aimed more at the female market.

Travelling steerage in a Ford dickey seat

The dickey seat – or rumble seat, as the Americans called it – was a feature of basic two-seat open cars right through until the 1930s. But with the closed saloon having become the standard body style, this type of coachwork was progressively disappearing.

Over in the United States, however, there was still a fondness for this auxiliary seating in the boot, and the British branch of the Ford Motor Company continued to offer the body type for a while on the American V8 models it sold – in relatively small numbers – in Britain. The photo shows a Type 40 Ford V8, these being imported from Ford's plant in Cork. Assembly of the V8 began at Dagenham in 1935, and roughly 12,500 of all types had been made by the time production stopped in 1940 – including a 'woody' shooting brake that did much to popularise the estate car in the United Kingdom.

Comfort was never a strong point for those seated in the dickey. You sat right over the rear axle, which was hard on the backside, and had no weather protection – although a variety of hoods and capes was offered by optimistic accessory manufacturers. Access was generally aided by two steps. These can be seen on this photo, one between the petrol tank and the rear wing, and one in the form of a rubber pad on top of the rear wing itself.

The 'trike' – economy with a sporting touch

Three-wheeled cars have long been a British peculiarity, and one nurtured by a quirk in legislation (now amended) whereby a three-wheeler of under 8 cwt counted as a 'motor tricycle' and could be driven on a motorcycle licence, with in addition a lower rate of road tax being payable.

In the inter-war period, the best-known 'trike' was the Morgan. Powered for most of its 1910–52 currency by motorcycle engines of one sort or another, the Morgan was a crude if sporting device. More civilised was the BSA three-wheeler of 1929–36 shown in this photo. Initially powered by a V-twin engine, with a four-cylinder power unit arriving for 1933, the BSA's most unusual feature was its use of front-wheel drive.

With or without front-wheel drive, a three-wheeler with its single wheel at the rear was always more stable than one with the single wheel at the front. Notwithstanding this, the dominant British-made 'trikes' made after the Second World War, the Bond and the Reliant, had their single wheel at the front – inevitably compromising their safety. Both sold in reasonable numbers to marginal motorists during the 1950s, in particular former motorcyclists who did not have a car licence, but by the 1960s their appeal was waning. The last Reliant three-wheeler was made in 2002, by which time the cars had become something of a national joke. Since then the genre has seen a revival, with Morgan bringing back a 'trike' in 2011.

Practising for the test in a Singer Bantam

It was only in 1935 that it became compulsory to take a driving test before being able to hold a full licence, and that 'L' plates for learners became obligatory. Until then, anyone could apply for a licence at a Post Office. The new requirement was not retrospective, so existing licence-holders did not have to take a test.

The driving test was suspended from 2 September 1939 until 1 November 1946, and in 1947 a period of one year was granted for wartime provisional licences to be converted to full licences without the need to pass the test.

Hand signals ceased to be demanded in 1975, but otherwise the test remained broadly the same until 1996, when a written theory examination was introduced; this was updated to a computer format in 2000, and two years later a computerised hazard-perception test was added. Various other changes have been made since. The booklet-type licence was replaced by a computerised folded slip in 1973, and this gave way to a photocard in 1999.

This photo shows racing-driver Victoria Worsley, who had at the time been a Ministry of Transport instructor for nine months, during which period her business had conducted nearly 2,000 tests. The car is a 9 hp Singer Bantam.

DRIVING TEST

SCHOOL OF
MOTORING

L

OFFICIAL
INSTRUCTION CAR

RING SPEEDWELL 3151

BDU 45

Garage selling British Coal Petrol

During the 1930s the Shell-Pratt's duopoly in petrol gave way to a more competitive environment, underpinned by strong advertising and more colourful filling stations with differently shaped 'globes' on top of the pumps. Makes such as Power, Dominion and Cleveland went on sale; meanwhile, Russian Oil Products started marketing ROP petrol. In 1931 the brand accounted for 14 per cent of sales, but this had crashed to 2 per cent by 1939.

There was another game in town, however: benzole, a fuel distilled from coal tar. Produced since early in the century, it had first been pushed in 1913, when a Petrol Substitutes Joint Committee was set up and *The Motor* organised trials and campaigns for this home-produced fuel. Production soared during the First World War, and afterwards, in 1919, the AA began propagandising for its adoption. Eventually Britain's producers came together to form the National Benzole Company, and by 1930 its benzole and petrol mix was the fourth-best seller in the country. A rival was Coalene 'British Coal Petrol' from Carless, Capel & Leonard, which was sold from nearly 200 pumps in 1936.

Whatever the fuel, it was taxed, as it had been since 1909, with the exception of a tax-free period from 1920 to 1928. In the latter year a 4d per gallon tax (21.3 per cent) was introduced, doubling to 8d a gallon in 1931 and rising to 9d a gallon (47.4 per cent) in 1938; this last hike made the price 1s 7d a gallon.

Loading the boot of a 'Flying' Standard

Up until the second half of the 1930s most cars did not have a separate boot: instead there was a folding luggage grid – often an extra-cost option – to which one could strap a trunk. Indeed, it was quite common for holidaying motorists to send their luggage ahead, despatching a trunk or trunks by train, to be collected by the hotel from the local station, along with guests arriving by railway. Such operations were often carried out in a multi-seater utility vehicle, hence the phrase 'station wagon'.

All this started to change with the arrival of more streamlined styles in the latter half of the 1930s, the longer tails of such designs allowing for a boot, often with an opening lid. Luggage lockers were hardly generous, however, and to make best use of the limited space many people bought fitted cases, tailored to suit the boot of a particular car.

Two such cases are here being slotted into the boot of a 'Flying' Standard – the streamlined range from the Coventry manufacturer introduced for 1936. This particular model is the V8, a short-lived variant with a 2868cc side-valve V8 engine. Rated at 20 hp, its annual road tax of £15 made it an unattractive proposition for the British motorist.

Enjoying the country in the most modern 'Ten'

This publicity image of an H-type Vauxhall Ten promotes the joys of leisure motoring, which was by the late 1930s far more of a reality. Not only had car prices fallen, but salaries had risen and paid holidays become vastly more widespread: more than 11 million Britons were entitled to holidays with pay by 1939, against 1.5 million in 1931.

Helping him profit from this additional leisure time, the British motorist of modest means had an increasing choice of serviceable family cars as the 1930s progressed. In particular, the Hillman Minx, followed by Tens from Austin, Morris and Ford, opened up a new class of 10 hp vehicle that soon came to replace the bigger and clumsier 12–14 hp cars that had previously been the market's centre of gravity. Sales of 9–10 hp cars jumped from 9 per cent of registrations in 1930 to 34 per cent in 1933.

Vauxhall was late to enter the contest. Purchased by General Motors in 1925, it took more than a decade to be transformed from a manufacturer of high-priced luxury cars into a generalist maker of affordable vehicles. The process was completed with the 1937 arrival of the 10 hp H-type. Not only that but the 'H', with its chassis-less unit construction, independent front suspension, hydraulic brakes, and pushrod engine, was arguably Britain's first modern motor car.

Accident on the Kingston by-pass

The Kingston by-pass, today's A3, was one of the main arterial roads out of London in the inter-war years, with roadhouses such as the Ace of Spades being well-known watering holes for motorists. With young blades, possibly a little tipsy, scorching out of town, perhaps down to Brooklands, accidents were inevitable; thankfully, third-party insurance had become obligatory in 1931.

At the time of this particular pile-up there was no speed limit prescribed for the by-pass, although a 30 mph limit had been in force since March 1935 in built-up areas, causing outrage in the motoring press. Astonishingly, the 20 mph overall limit for all roads, introduced in 1904, was only withdrawn at the beginning of 1931.

Helping educate motorists, the Highway Code was first published that same year; helping pedestrians, meanwhile, was the 1935 arrival of the first pedestrian crossings, with their 'Belisha Beacons' – named after Minister of Transport Leslie Hore-Belisha. Did all this reduce accidents? In 1928 – two years after the first automatic traffic lights had been introduced, at London's Piccadilly Circus – 6,138 people were killed and 164,838 injured on British roads. In 1935 the figures were 7,343 killed and 231,603 injured, representing increases of, respectively, 19.6 per cent and a rather more substantial 40.5 per cent. During that period, the number of cars on the road increased by 67.1 per cent: if the roads were getting more dangerous, it was not in direct proportion to the increase in the number of cars.

WVS canteen in Deptford, London

The Women's Volunteer Services (WVS), were an important part of the Home Front during the Second World War. One of the many contributions they made was to run mobile canteens in bombed-out areas. The vehicle shown is typical of the many converted from regular passenger cars, being based on a 1935–6 Type 68 Ford V8 saloon. Many such vehicles were converted into slightly odd-looking estate cars or 'utilities' after the war.

As well as matt paint, the car has one headlamp blanked out and the other carrying a mask, as required by blackout regulations; other lighting would also have had its output restricted by partial blanking-out. The bumpers and the edges of the wings and running-boards are white-painted, another stipulation, intended to aid visibility in the unlit streets of wartime Britain.

As might be imagined, motoring during the war was severely curtailed. Petrol was rationed within two weeks of the outbreak of hostilities, and in 1942 withdrawn totally for private motoring. That year there were only half a million cars on the roads, against 2.5 million in 1938; only those who could claim essential use were entitled to use their vehicle, so most were laid up on blocks 'for the duration'. Un-branded low-octane 'Pool' was available only to approved users such as emergency services, farmers and bus companies, and was dyed to identify unauthorised use.

The jam factory's armoured car

In 1940 the Secretary of State for War, Anthony Eden, announced the creation of the Local Defence Volunteers (LDV), better known as the Home Guard. Briefed to help defend Britain against possible German invasion, one of the Home Guard's many acts of improvisation was to convert old passenger vehicles into rudimentary armoured cars. This particular example – complete with worryingly bald front tyres – seems to be based on a mid-1930s American saloon, and was created by the Home Guard team of the St Martin Preserving Company, famous for its St Martin 'Chunky' marmalade; whether this was the Ely branch of the firm or the Maidenhead branch is not said in the caption to this Fox Photos image.

Other uses of old cars included their being employed as improvised fencing to prevent enemy planes landing in farmers' fields. In addition many cars were scrapped as part of the wartime drive for metal: in 1943 the government announced a plan to break a quarter of a million vehicles over 18 months for parts and for raw materials to recycle.

Purpose-built armoured cars on car chassis were made during the Second World War by Humber, as the Humberette and the Ironside, and by Standard, as the Beaverette. Luxuriously trimmed versions of the Ironside, which was based on the Humber Super Snipe, were used by the British royal family.

Gas-powered Austins in wartime Birmingham

With the withdrawal of petrol for private motoring in 1942, the only way to carry on motoring was to turn to an alternative power source. In France the favoured choice was to use a wood-burner to produce wood gas – a messy, convoluted and not hugely reliable process. In Britain, a less rural country with a greater availability of piped 'town gas', a more satisfactory arrangement was to convert one's car to run on gas, with a large flexible reservoir fitted to the car roof.

The photo shows two Austins operating as taxis and kitted out for town gas, which at the time was a by-product of converting coal to coke. Performance didn't suffer over-much, but the huge gas tanks perched on the roof made for ponderous handling. The reservoir, generally made of rubber-coated silk, would have given the car a range of 15–20 miles, or 30 miles at the very most.

Behind is a once-familiar sight, an electric tram. By 1935 these were starting to be phased out in favour of diesel buses and trolleybuses. In 1952 they were withdrawn entirely in London, and a year later in Birmingham. As for the trolleybus, Birmingham gave these up in 1951, but London continued to run them until 1962. Of late, the tram has started to make a return to city streets in Britain.

A less noble use for a Rolls-Royce

The notion of a Rolls-Royce tow truck might seem a heresy, but until the 1960s such sights were not uncommon. Rolls-Royces, particularly the smaller models, were often rebodied in later life as ambulances, hearses, shooting-brakes or – as here – breakdown trucks. Such cars might then have had a third lease of life as low-cost transport for the impecunious: the author recalls from his 1960s childhood the local tree surgeon, an eccentric recluse, motoring about Surrey in a van-bodied 20 hp Rolls-Royce.

The use of these fine motor cars in such a way was a tribute to their exquisitely high standards of engineering. The ash-framed bodies of the time might have had limited durability, but the mechanicals were indestructible. Additionally there was a moment when aged but low-mileage hearses were disposed of by funeral directors: with the wood interior removed, it wasn't complicated to arrive at a cheap and spacious estate car.

Survivors from such exercises eventually ended up in the hands of enthusiasts who sought to rebody them. With the cheapest-to-build and supposedly most desirable type being an open tourer, all too many reproduction open four-seaters exist today, giving a false impression of how most pre-1945 Rolls-Royces were originally bodied.

Branded petrol returns to Leatherhead garage

Petrol retailing has come a long way since June 1945, when the basic petrol ration was reintroduced. The allocation was increased in 1946, but the following year withdrawn entirely, to save foreign exchange. After vigorous protests, in 1948 'basic' was reintroduced, but with an entitlement to only a third as much as before; meanwhile petrol dyed red was available for commercial vehicles, it being an offence to use this for private motoring. Only in May 1950 did petrol come off-ration, but the fuel was still 'Pool' petrol of at best a 74-octane rating.

Branded petrol, in three grades, returned in 1953, and soon better-quality fuels became available, such as BP Super petrol – 'for more energy per gallon' – introduced in 1955. By 1960 98-octane petrol was available, and during the 1960s 'five-star' 101-octane fuel came onto the market. Publicity became slicker, and petrol companies vied with each other for the most preposterous or just plain fatuous adverts.

Until the 1960s you had an attendant pumping the petrol into your car. Shell opened its first self-service station in 1963, two years ahead of Mobil, and the idea was still a relative novelty at the beginning of the 1970s: in 1972 there were just 1,500 self-service stations in Britain, out of a total of 38,000 outlets. Apart from reducing staffing costs, self-service was also found to increase the value of the average fill, so by the 1980s it had, unsurprisingly, become the norm.

OPEN
8·0 AM TO 6·0 PM

Enduring favourite – the Minor Traveller

After the war a profusion of wood-framed estate cars appeared. Such vehicles allowed smaller manufacturers who had limited body-making capacity to clothe their chassis in a convenient and economic way. They were also briefly in vogue, until the loophole was closed in 1947, as a means of dodging Purchase Tax – this not initially being payable on cars with so-called 'utility' bodies.

Small estate cars came to be offered by some of the bigger manufacturers, but they were essentially converted vans. The Morris Minor Traveller, launched in October 1953, was the first not spun off from a light commercial vehicle. That it still had an external ash frame and part-aluminium panelling meant that tooling costs for an all-steel body were avoided, and suggest that Morris envisaged relatively limited sales in what doubtless seemed an uncertain new sector of the market: after all, it was only in 1950 that a legally woolly 30 mph speed limit for 'utility' vehicles had been lifted.

Sweet to drive and spacious, the Minor Traveller was a continuing sales success throughout its long life, and is still a much-loved vehicle. Approximately 215,000 made were made – about 13 per cent of the 1.6 million Minors churned out between 1948 and 1972. Indeed, in later years the Traveller accounted for over 40 per cent of Minor output. Unfortunately the labour-intensive wood-framed body meant that the Traveller apparently never made money, as its retail price did not reflect the substantially higher labour and materials costs.

AA patrolman on the A5 trunk road

A familiar institution almost since the beginning of motoring, the Automobile Association (AA) was founded in 1905 – some years after its rival, the Royal Automobile Club (RAC). It was established to protect and advance the interests of motorists – and, more specifically, to patrol roads and warn members of speed traps.

Its role rapidly expanded into the areas of legal defence, insurance and help with foreign touring, as well as hotel grading, but it was only in 1919 that it initiated its 'mechanical first aid' scheme, with patrolmen on motorcycle combinations equipped to cope with breakdowns. Another critical contribution was the erection of signposts and village signs around the country. By 1939 the AA had 725,000 members, representing about a third of Britain's motorists; in 1950 the figure reached a million, and by 1973, in which year the Relay recovery scheme was introduced, membership was just over 5.1 million.

It was only in 1962 that patrolmen were no longer required to salute a member: originally the absence of a salute was intended as an indication that there was a speed trap ahead. Another landmark was the 1968 abandonment of the AA's motorcycle combinations. In 1999 the AA became a private limited company; a separate AA Motoring Trust operates as a lobbying and research body, in much the same way as does the RAC Foundation.

Land Rover as racing-car transporter, Crystal Palace

Few vehicles can have had a greater and longer-lived impact on British life than the Land Rover. Truly the most multi-purpose of cars, it has served as everything from warhorse to royal procession vehicle, and in every corner of the world. But its principal role, for which it was conceived, was as a vehicle for the farmer.

At the end of the Second World War, farm mechanisation was a priority. Simultaneously, Rover was struggling, as allocations of rationed steel to make cars were made by the government on the basis of export performance. The company, having largely catered to the home market, could only expect limited allocations.

However, aluminium was more readily available, and so it was decided – purely as a stop-gap – to make a Jeep-like vehicle for the British farmer, using aluminium panelling for a simple body demanding minimal tooling, and with a chassis cheaply welded up from sheets of steel. With four-wheel drive as standard, and a handy power take-off, the Land Rover was a nimble, affordable maid-of-all-work. An immediate success, any thought of it being rapidly discontinued soon evaporated.

This mildly customised example is serving as a transporter for the Formula 3 Cooper of racing driver Stuart Lewis-Evans.

Launch of UK-built Isetta, Dorchester Hotel, London

The bubble car became a quirky part of the British motoring scene in the late 1950s, largely as a result of the 1956–7 Suez Crisis and the temporary imposition of petrol rationing: a fuel consumption of 60 mpg was not without appeal. The two makes that defined the genre were the Isetta (made by BMW but originally an Italian design) and the Heinkel – the latter also assembled in Britain as the Trojan.

The two cars shared the feature of a front that hinged open as the sole door, and the Heinkel boasted a bench seat for children at the rear, something made possible by its extra foot of length relative to the Isetta. Both had single-cylinder engines, of 250cc or 300cc for the Isetta and 175cc or 200cc for the Heinkel. This made for limited and noisy performance, and the cars required a certain knack to drive.

The photo shows an Isetta at the 1957 announcement of the impending start of British manufacture. Built in Brighton, the cars mainly had a single rear wheel, to meet 'motor tricycle' legislation, whereas Isettas made elsewhere had two close-set rear wheels.

Although some were undoubtedly used as family cars, most were bought as city runabouts or second cars, and were by no means an unusual sight on the roads of Britain, well into the 1960s. But once the Mini had established itself, there was no call for such minimalist vehicles.

Early seat belt promotion at Hendon Aerodrome

Safety was a rarely discussed issue in the 1950s, so when the first seat belts made their appearance it was a newsworthy event. In this October 1957 photo, future 'Dr Who' Jon Pertwee, described as a 'well-known radio and television personality', is seen adjusting the Swedish-made RKN safety harness worn by twenty-year-old fashion model Rita Royce, as part of a Safe Driving Competition organised at Hendon Aerodrome by the Hendon and Finchley Road Safety Committee. The car is a real rarity – a Daimler Conquest roadster, of which only sixty-five were made, between 1953 and 1955.

Seat belts of the modern three-point type were first fitted as standard to a mainstream car by Volvo in 1959 – following Saab's introduction of belts the previous year on its limited-production GT750. Attachment points became compulsory in Britain in 1965, and the fitment of belts in 1967, backdated a year later to all cars built since the beginning of 1965. The wearing of belts only became a legal requirement in 1983, after much impassioned debate about personal liberties. Rear seat belts had to be fitted from 1986, and children were required to wear the belts from 1989; in 1991 the universal use of rear belts became compulsory.

Other keynote road safety legislation in the past half-century includes the permanent imposition of a 70 mph speed limit in 1967, after a trial beginning in 1965, and the introduction of breathalyser testing, also in 1967.

Forecourt at a London car dealer

During the 1950s the government adopted a 'stop-go' approach to the economy, regularly adjusting interest rates and taxation to control spending. In 1947 a double Purchase Tax of 66.6 per cent had been introduced on cars with a pre-tax price of £1,000 or more; this was then abandoned in 1950, only to be reimposed in 1951, but this time on all cars. In 1953 the tax was reduced to 50 per cent, but then increased to 60 per cent in 1958.

The industry was also obliged by the government to export the greater part of its output, to gain foreign exchange. This pressure to export was only gradually relaxed, so waiting lists for new cars remained long for much of the decade: it is telling that it was only in 1955 that *The Autocar* saw fit to publish a list of the prices of new cars. Second-hand vehicles thus remained at a premium, with nearly new cars selling for more than their list price.

By 1958 the economy was less tightly bound. That year hire purchase restrictions were lifted. With output of new cars not meeting demand, sales of second-hand vehicles boomed. Alas, the economy was soon overheating, and in 1960 a credit squeeze was initiated; only in 1962 were restraints on credit lifted and Purchase Tax reduced – in two stages – to 25 per cent. The brakes were off the motor industry, and the increasingly prosperous British motorist was at last able to walk into a showroom and buy the car he wanted.

Goggomobil Mayfair coupé receives a ticket

With worsening traffic densities in London, the first parking meters arrived in July 1958, sparking a wave of hostility towards Minister of Transport Ernest Marples, who soon became the victim of 'Marples Must Go' car-window stickers. Eventually there would be approximately 750,000 meters across Britain.

Half a century later there were 4,300 meters in Central London alone, and the City of Westminster had taken the decision to replace them – during 2009 – with paid parking by chip-and-pin and mobile phone. One reason was that rival Albanian gangs were fighting for control of master keys to sets of meters, and the council was losing up to £120,000 a week to these thieves. At the time, it cost £4 for an hour's parking, against the 6 shillings the driver of this Goggomobil would have paid. The fine for overstaying, £2 in 1958, had risen to £120 fifty years later, or £60 for prompt payment.

Since 1991 councils have had the power to enforce parking regulations themselves; until then it had been the responsibility of the police and courts. The work of traffic wardens, previously employed by the councils, has been sub-contracted to private firms. With incentive schemes for armies of privatised wardens, and instantaneous electronic ticketing, parking has become a major revenue source for local authorities: in 2009 councils raised £1.3 billion from parking tickets and fines. Unsurprisingly, motorists have increasingly found themselves having to appeal against tickets issued unreasonably.

Mr Giles and his old Ford van

Tradesmen delivering to villages were very much a part of rural life, and remained so into the 1960s. Inevitably they turned to motor transport, not least the light vans offered by Ford and, from 1923, by Morris. By 1938 there were over 200,000 commercial vehicles of less than 1½ tons payload on British roads. That said, horse-carts were still a common sight in pre-war Britain, and even into the early post-war years: in 1934 a census revealed 131,000 freight horses still in service.

This 1957 photo shows eighty-three-year-old Mr W. Giles, described as a familiar figure around Winchcombe in Gloucestershire. Mr Giles had been delivering paraffin and household goods to local villages for over fifty years – originally by horse and cart, rather than with the 1920s Ford Model T van seen here.

With the final consolidation of car ownership across all classes and income groups in the 1960s, people took to driving to town for their shopping. This inevitably led to the disappearance both of village shops and of grocers' delivery services and travelling tradesmen. The last vestiges of this practice are Britain's milkmen, traditionally delivering – in urban areas at least – by electric milk-float.

Lotus Seven at London DIY show

Britain has always been accommodating to enthusiasts wishing to build their own cars, and in the late 1950s and early 1960s a whole industry existed to supply kits of parts to convert old Ford Eights and Tens and Austin Sevens into often rudimentary sports cars, with modified suspension and braking, a glassfibre or aluminium body, and perhaps even a new chassis. Eventually the mechanicals of the Fords and Austins started to look hopelessly outdated, and with the arrival of cheap second-hand mainstream sports cars the demand for these kit cars evaporated.

Colin Chapman, creator of the Lotus company, began by making and racing Austin Seven specials. His first production model was the Lotus Six. This was a simple kit of a tubular frame and a minimalist body, to which the customer fitted his own mechanical parts. Most were used for low-level 'Clubman' racing. Chapman sought to replace the Six with a more sophisticated model that could tap into the market for kit cars as well as serving as a club racer. The result, launched in 1957, was the Lotus Seven, of which an early example is shown here. Built around a lightweight tubular spaceframe and using a mix of BMC and Ford mechanicals, depending on specification, it was said that the car could be assembled at home in 30–60 hours, for less than £600. The Seven is still in production, as the Caterham.

M1 motorway on its day of opening

Schemes for road systems – ambitious, grandiose or sometimes downright fantastical – were a part of motoring discourse right from Edwardian times. Yet between 1924 and 1937 a mere 1,600 miles of new road was built in the United Kingdom. In the latter year Hitler's Germany had over 800 miles of dual-carriageway autobahn in operation; it was to take Britain until 1971 to have its first 800 miles of motorway.

One of the few new highways was that linking Liverpool and Manchester, inaugurated in 1933 – a year in which the government claimed that there were 220 by-passes in operation. The following year London's North Circular was finally completed, and in 1939 the Winchester by-pass boasted the country's first flyovers. This was progress at a snail's pace: in 1938 there were just 27.5 miles of dual carriageway in Britain.

The first stretch of motorway only arrived in 1958, with the completion of the Preston by-pass, now part of the M6. The first full-blown motorway, the M1, opened the following year – to much excitement and a certain amount of drama, as all too many motorists, unused to sustained high speeds, ended up on the hard shoulder with an expiring motor car.

This foot-dragging continued into modern times. The M25 London orbital, planning of which took up much of the 1960s, was only completed in 1986, after approaching forty public enquiries, and once in operation was unable to cope with the volume of traffic it attracted.

The Mini changes the face of motoring

The Mini created a revolution in British motoring. Technically, the use of an engine set crossways and driving the front wheels set the template for the majority of today's cars. More specifically, it allowed four seats to be fitted into a vehicle just 10 feet long – an extraordinary achievement.

Cheeky, practical and low-priced, the Mini was intended to be a riposte to the bubble cars of the late-1950s, but ended up as much more. It helped complete the motorisation of a newly prosperous Britain, but also became popular across all social classes, not least after the sporting Cooper variant was introduced in 1961. The Mini became emblematic of a Britain that was shedding its old-fashioned fustiness and its rigid social stratification. It became associated with Swinging London and The Beatles, but also became a giant-killing rally winner.

In production until 2000, it made little or no money for its makers, thanks to poor initial costing, relative mechanical complexity, expensive rectifications under warranty in the early years, and dwindling production in later decades. But virtually every family in England has had experience of the Mini, and even today the go-kart joys of driving that little shoebox on wheels remain undiminished.

Renault Dauphine minicab and Austin FX3 taxi

Minicabs are today such a part of motoring that it is difficult to believe that they are a relatively recent innovation – and one that originally provoked controversy and even violence. The first were put on the road in 1961, notably by London car dealer Welbeck Motors. The fleet of red-painted Renault Dauphines could not ply for hire, as they were not licensed by Scotland Yard. An advanced booking had to be made, but what constituted such a booking was open to interpretation.

The black-cab trade was swiftly up in arms, and minicab drivers found themselves boxed in by taxi drivers; minicabs were vandalised, and in some instances even overturned. Some taxi drivers were jailed for acts of intimidation; there was a two-day taxi strike. Welbeck subsidised costs by having advertising on the cars – Air France, as on this Welbeck Dauphine, being a major sponsor. But as the dispute became uglier, advertisers withdrew their support.

Despite all this, by early 1962 there were thirty-odd minicab firms in London, but heady talk of having 5,000 minicabs operating in the capital ultimately translated into a mere 200 on the roads by the beginning of 1963. Since then, the minicab has gradually – if grudgingly – become accepted, but it was only in the 1990s that a licensing system was introduced, for London only. According to the National Private Hire Association, in 2014 there were 52,691 minicabs in service in London and 157,307 in England and Wales as a whole.

End of the road for 'old bangers'

At the end of the 1950s pre-war cars were still a common sight. This was partly because, for much of the decade, new cars had been difficult to obtain, but also because they had remained unaffordable for much of the motoring public. With greater productivity, a lessening emphasis on exports, and growing prosperity in Britain, this was starting to change, and older vehicles were moving down the automotive food chain, with inevitable concerns about the roadworthiness of cars that were twenty years old or more. So it was that in February 1961 the Ministry of Transport introduced the so-called 'Ten-Year Test' for all cars over ten years old.

The arrival of what became known as the MoT test led to scrapyards being flooded with pre-war vehicles. In the month of the test's introduction the Motor Vehicle Dismantlers' Association (MVDA) said that its 250 members were breaking up to 4,000 cars a week and could not cope with such volumes. Dumped cars would also become a growing problem during the 1960s: in 1964 it was reported that over 6,000 vehicles were being abandoned in Britain every year.

In the photo of this scrapyard, at Waltham Cross in Hertfordshire, all the cars visible are of pre-war type. The car suspended in the air is an Austin Eight, as made between 1939 and 1947.

The Met unveils its Humber patrol cars

With the arrival of the motorway, the police realised that they would need capacious and high-performing cars to patrol the new roads. Ford Zephyr MkII estates soon became the default choice, and big Ford estates remained popular right through to Granada days. Another 1960s option was the Humber Super Snipe estate, favoured by constabularies such as those of Kent, Northamptonshire and Hertfordshire.

In 1961 the Metropolitan Police turned to Humber and their 'Specially Equipped Traffic Accident Car' (SETAC), shown here. Equipment included flashing signals, jacks for lifting heavy loads, floodlights, and of course a loudhailer. The Met also famously used a total of twenty-six Daimler SP250 sports cars for high-speed duties.

Patrols offered assistance and advice, and responded to accidents, but in the early days of the motorways there were no speed limits to enforce. On the other hand the police had to cope with motorists unused to the new highways, and who sometimes indulged in dangerous manoeuvres. These included U-turns, and stopping by the side of the inside lane – this in the days before crash-barriered central reservations and hard shoulders had been introduced. Unsurprisingly, a film on motorway discipline was soon commissioned to educate the public.

A family outing by Ford Cortina

The arrival of the Ford Cortina in 1962 was a transformational event – technically, industrially, and in terms of the socio-economics of British motoring. It became a national institution, being produced in four different guises up until 1982, by which time approaching 4.3 million had been made. Its departure prompted a TV documentary, and at least forty songs feature the Cortina in the title or the lyrics.

The secret of the original Cortina was a carefully calculated lightweight bodyshell that used the minimum of metal. This drove down manufacturing costs, which in turn allowed a larger car to be offered for the same money being asked for smaller but heavier saloons from rival manufacturers. For a British motorist looking for spacious family transport at a low price, the Cortina was the answer to his prayers: cars such as the Hillman Minx and Austin Cambridge suddenly looked old-fashioned, overweight, cramped, and needlessly expensive. Helping sales along was a roomy estate, which in up-market Super form, as shown here, initially featured a splash of pure Americana – imitation-wood side trim in machine-printed Di-Noc.

Equally to the point, in a British market where fleet sales of 'company cars' were a more important part of the mix than in any other European country, the Cortina soon achieved an easy dominance. Its transatlantic-tinged looks appealed to status-hungry sales reps, who also appreciated its sizeable boot, while fleet managers valued its conventional, easy-maintenance rear-drive mechanicals.

Two ladies and a Riley Kestrel

Women have featured in advertising and in PR photos since the dawn of motoring, but it would be a mistake to believe that lady motorists rapidly became an important part of British life. Despite advertisements regularly being aimed at lady drivers from at least the 1920s, in 1933 only 12 per cent of licences were held by women and even as late as 1968 fewer than 40 per cent of those taking the driving test were female.

Since the 1960s the number of women driving has increased significantly. Indeed, a 2012 survey by the RAC Foundation found that the number of women with a licence had grown by 23 per cent between 1995 and 2010, against a 9 per cent rise for men. This has meant that the imbalance between the sexes is disappearing: in 2010 there were 16.3 million male and 13.8 million female licence holders.

Whether one of the ladies in this publicity photo would have chosen the Riley Kestrel herself, or relied on the decision of the pipe-smoking husband who was still a fixture in advertising at the time, she would have been one of many to enjoy a car from BMC's 1100/1300 range. Launched in 1962, the original 1100 was the most advanced small/medium car in the world, offering comfort, space and Mini-like handling. Along with derivatives such as the Riley, it was for many years Britain's best-selling range of cars, and at times held nearly 15 per cent of the market, an extraordinary feat for a single model.

Holidaying in a Bedford Dormobile

There have been motor-caravans (or camper-vans) since the dawn of motoring, but as a production vehicle made in other than the very smallest of numbers the breed only came into being in the 1950s. This was due to the arrival of various forward-control or semi-forward-control light vans that lent themselves to conversion. In Britain the first modern van of this type was the 1952–69 Bedford CA, a semi-forward-control design with the engine protruding slightly into the cab.

Kent coachbuilder Martin Walter was the first to see the opportunity offered by the Bedford, and began making basic sleeper-van conversions under the Dormobile name – one that soon became a generic term for motor-caravans. By the beginning of the 1960s there were seventeen UK manufacturers. Martin Walter was, however, by far the market leader, its Dormobile conversions being readily identifiable by the side-hinged, glassfibre elevating roof featured on most models from 1957 onwards. In 1969 over 5,000 motorvans were sold. Roughly 1,700 were Dormobiles, based not just on Bedfords but also on the forward-control Ford, BMC, Commer and VW vans; this layout, in which the engine was fully within the envelope of a flat-fronted body, was especially practical.

Some motor-vans had fully coachbuilt bodies but the majority retained the basic bodyshell of the van in question, as in the case of the Bedford-based Dormobile Romany depicted here. Accommodation in this instance was either two single beds or a double bed 'below decks' and a pair of hammock bunks in the elevating roof.

Capri – the car with the 'Custom Plan'

By the end of the 1960s the 'consumer society' was very much a reality, and cars were regarded with a less utilitarian eye. For some buyers style and making a statement counted for more than notions of interior space or technical prowess. Ford, having made a huge success of its Mustang 'personal car' in the United States, sought to repeat the exercise in Europe with the Capri.

In many ways a shrunken Mustang, the Capri had a sleek, long-bonnet coupé body over what were essentially Ford Cortina mechanicals. Interior accommodation was no better – in fact probably worse – than that of the smaller Ford Escort, but the Capri gave dads with family responsibilities the chance to stick with a sporty motor car for a few more years.

The Capri, billed as 'the car you always promised yourself', was also important in that it introduced to the British motorist the possibility of customising his vehicle by ordering different permutations of various trim packs – instead of, as previously, being faced by a bald choice between, say, a De Luxe model and a slightly more posh Super. In theory the buyer of a Capri could choose between any combination of three packs – 'X', 'L' and 'R' – as well as a whole range of engines, from 1300cc to 3000cc. In practice, Ford realised it had needlessly complicated manufacture, and pushed purchasers towards the 'L', 'XL' and 'XLR' specifications, which soon became the sole choices.

Original Range Rover starts a fashion

The face of British motoring began to change with the 1970 arrival of the Range Rover. One of British Leyland's rare success stories, it had been created by the Rover company as an all-wheel-drive dual-purpose vehicle less spartan than the Land Rover. With its comfortable long-stroke suspension and smooth V8 engine, the Range Rover was adapted by well-to-do country folk as an alternative to a traditional estate car, and soon town dwellers were following suit, even if they had no use for a hefty four-wheel-drive utility vehicle.

A fashion had been launched. With BL unable to meet demand, Japanese manufacturers started to market 4x4s in Britain, helpfully slotting into the price gap between the modestly priced but crude Land Rover and the sophisticated but ever more expensive Range Rover. Since the 1980s the demand for what are now termed Sports Utility Vehicles, or SUVs, has soared. By 1994 the breed was accounting for 3.7 per cent of the British market. Nine years later that had risen to 6.2 per cent. In 2013 the figure was 11 per cent, and no manufacturer can afford not to have at least one SUV in its range.

Progressively, these 4x4s have become more sporting, and less utilitarian, and have steadily contributed to making the conventional estate car a less common sight on British roads – even if such a vehicle would be a more spacious and more fuel-efficient choice for the average motorist.

Unsold cars at BL's Cowley plant

This photo aptly sums up British motoring at the turn of the 1980s: a stockyard of British Leyland cars not motoring anywhere. At its formation in 1968, BL controlled 40 per cent of the British market. When this photo was taken in February 1980, the company's market share had fallen to 15 per cent.

The nation's private car buyers did not want to buy the firm's products. Quality was poor, supply was patchy as a result of constant strikes, and too many of the cars were of dated or unsatisfactory design. The Princesses in the foreground of the photo had been launched in 1975 to a good reception by the press, but quality and reliability issues torpedoed sales; in 1980 just 14,612 would be made.

The British motorist was a more cosmopolitan consumer than those in many countries, and turned sooner to foreign cars: it is instructive to see the progressive rise in sales of Saabs and Volvos during the 1960s. The arrival of well-equipped and conscientiously manufactured Japanese cars in the early 1970s was, however, the real game changer; also influential was the lowering of tariffs on European cars following Britain's joining in 1973 of what was then called the European Economic Community (EEC). Faced with a choice of readily available imported cars of demonstrably better quality, the private buyer turned his back on the frequently shoddy domestic product, changing forever the face of British motoring. In 1977 imports for the first time exceeded 50 per cent of the market.

Peugeot 806 'people carrier'

The traditional estate was further threatened by the 1980s arrival of the 'people carrier' or Multi-Purpose Vehicle (MPV). The Renault Espace of 1984 set the template: a spacious interior often with a third row of seats, made possible by moving the passenger compartment forward and having a taller body with more upright seating.

Unlike SUVs, which for most users have no practical advantages over a regular estate, 'people-carriers' make family motoring more agreeable, offering a roomy multi-configurational interior with folding and/or removable seats, the opportunity to carry a tribe of children around, and a commanding driving position.

With the boom in outdoor activities, the advantages of a family car that can happily accommodate mountain bikes, sailboards and other paraphernalia are evident. With MPVs now in varying sizes, a UK market share of 0.7 per cent in 1994 rose to 6.7 per cent in 2013.

Speed cameras – part of driving today

One invention that has changed the face of British motoring is the speed camera, commonly known as a 'Gatso' after its inventor, Dutch former rally-driver Maurice Gatsonides. The first cameras were installed in 1992, and by 2007 there were close to 5,000 fixed cameras in the UK, as well as countless temporary installations alongside motorway roadworks. A relatively recent addition at these locations – and elsewhere – has been the gantry-mounted, average-speed camera. Bus lanes in cities are also monitored by camera, as are certain traffic lights.

The safety benefits of speed cameras have been much debated, but statistics confirm their effectiveness. However, while few would argue about siting a speed camera close to a school, for example, some would judge certain cameras to be located purely where they have the greatest chance of generating revenue. This view has had greater credibility since 2000, when local authorities were allowed to keep a proportion of camera income: camera numbers nearly trebled in seven years, and trigger-speeds were in some instances reduced. In 2007, in which year the system was reformed, 1.8 million motorists were caught by speed camera, representing perhaps £100 million in fines.

Avoiding being flashed by a camera, identifying and keeping out of bus lanes that have differing times of operation, slowing down to the 20 mph speed limit now operational in some parts of the country, suffering the car-jarring effects of speed humps: in the past few years driving has become more of a discipline and less of a pleasure.

Toyota Prius hybrid

Ever since the passing of the first legislation in the US, in 1967, the control of vehicle emissions has been an issue of progressively increasing significance. Today, more than ever, the environmental impact of the car occupies the minds of NGOs, governments and automotive engineers, even though private cars account for just 13.4 per cent of the UK's carbon dioxide emissions, against the 40.7 per cent accounted for by energy production, according to figures provided by the Society of Motor Manufacturers and Traders (SMMT).

Limiting noxious exhaust emissions led initially to more sophisticated fuel systems and more efficient combustion, but also to the obligatory fitting of catalysts from August 1992 and the withdrawal of leaded petrol in 2000. Currently the pressure is to reduce carbon dioxide emissions.

On one hand this has led to a race to register ever-lower CO_2 figures according to an EU testing regime that may well be more meaningful in theory than in practice. On the other hand it has prompted the marketing of electric and hybrid – or part-electric – vehicles. With their high cost and restricted range, the former have yet to make any impact. With no 'range anxiety' issues, the more affordable hybrids are, however, becoming a common sight. Whether they – or improved electric cars – will become the norm in decades to come, as many predict, remains to be seen. If so, the face of motoring truly will have changed, not least on account of the complexity and higher price of such vehicles.

MGs at a rally in Windsor

No overview of motoring in Britain would be complete without a mention of the world of historic vehicles. This is more vibrant and deeper-rooted than in any other European country. The British were the first to define the three categories that identify the oldest vehicles: 'veteran' for cars made before 1905, 'vintage' for cars made after 1918 and before 1931, and 'Edwardian' for those cars made in between. The preservation and use of such vehicles was encouraged by the formation of the Veteran Car Club in 1930 and the Vintage Sports-Car Club in 1934.

During the 1960s two further strands emerged. First, with the scrapping of so many pre-war cars in the wake of the 1961 introduction of the MoT test, people started to band together to preserve post-1930 cars. Then, towards the end of the decade, magazines started talking about 'the vintage cars of tomorrow' and identifying post-1945 cars worthy of preservation. This movement gathered pace slowly – the notion that anyone might want to restore and molly-coddle a 1930s Morris Eight, for example, was aberrant to the older generation of enthusiast.

The launch of the magazine *Classic Car* in 1973 marked the coming of age of the 'classic car' movement, and across Europe there is now agreement that any car over thirty years old counts as 'historic'. According to a 2011 survey, historic motoring in Britain encompasses over 850,000 vehicles, employs 28,000 people across 4,000 businesses and museums, and contributes £4 billion annually to the economy.

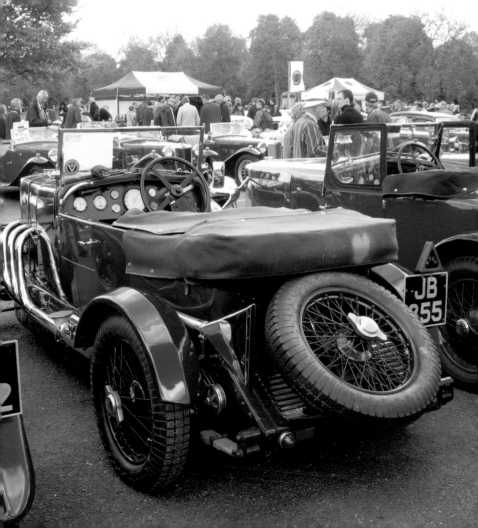

A note on horsepower and taxation

References to cars being of a certain 'hp' – or of being called an 'Eight' or a 'Ten' for example – are a reflection on the vehicle's horsepower rating for taxation purposes, as used for the Road Tax between 1910 and 1947. This fiscal horsepower should not be confused with brake horsepower. The 'hp' rating of a car was arrived at by a mathematical formula devised by the RAC, whereby the determining factor was the engine's bore. The system was revised in 1921, with cars being taxed annually at a rate of £1 per horsepower, a move intended to discourage the purchase of larger-engined cars of American origin. The rate was reduced to 15s per hp in 1935 but increased to £1 5s 0d for 1940, in which year Purchase Tax was also introduced, on all new cars. In 1947 the horsepower tax was scrapped in favour of a flat rate for all cars regardless of horsepower rating or engine capacity. In 1999 a two-tier Vehicle Excise Duty was introduced, with different rates for cars of below and above 1100cc; in 2005 this was replaced by a graduated rating based on CO_2 emissions.

Acknowledgements

Images on pages 31, 63, 83, 91, 97, 99, 103 and 109 are from the author's collection, that on page 13 was kindly supplied by David Burgess-Wise, and that on page 107 is courtesy Toyota (GB). All other photos are from the Getty Images archive; grateful thanks to Amba Horton and Caroline and Catherine Theakstone for their assistance.